Dew-Drops Of The Soul

D0796959

By

Yogiraj Gurunath

Alight Publications

2001

Dew-Drops of the Soul

By Yogiraj Gurunath

First Edition Published in December, 2001

Alight Publications
PO Box 930
Union City, CA 94587

http://www.i-Alight.com

ISBN 1-931833-00-1

Printed in the United States of America

This is a unique compilation of nineteen poetic gems from a contemporary Himalayan Master, a Self-realized and perfected Being, whom we call Yogiraj Sat-Gurunath.

Gurunath has often mentioned that these " Dew Drops of the Soul" express the essence of his inner experience and that they are the best source to learn the heights and depths of Yoga.

These "Dewdrops" are simply written in the unique way that Gurunath is able to capture the sublime in a down to earth manner for us to better understand the non-describable nature of reality.

Gurunath speaks to the soul through the doorway of the heart. He opens up our hearts so that we can attune ourselves to the reality of the True Self, in spite of the limitations of the human language and through many guises of our day-to-day experience.

Twelve of the nineteen poems are appearing in print for the first time, while seven of them have been previously published in "Anubhuti" [1997; India]

For those of you who want to know more about Gurunath, you will find valuable information in the Appendix.

Turn to the "Dewdrops" and take flight on the back of the soaring Hamsa Soul-Swan.

Sat Gurunath Maharaj Ki Jay !

Editor
Runbir Singh
[Rudra Shivananda]

Table of Contents

Dew Drops of the Soul

Death

Why do people think of me,
What I am not supposed to be?
Death's cold hand they often say,
Will snatch away your earthly stay.

They call me Death and yet
I take them to eternity.
Oh this paradox of Ignorance
Deludes humanity.

Men steeped in earthly ignorance
Do dread me as their foe
Knowing not that to their Souls
The light of truth I show.

Ye Sons of Light, I am not night
Of darkness and despair
I come to save you from your woes,
Your worries and your cares.

To take you to the stillness
And that peace you often craved
That plenitude of quietude,
Land of the pure and brave.

Yogiraj Gurunath

I am the one and only way
To reach the goal sublime
Pass through my gates of Death you must
To meet your Lord Divine.

Then shun me not ye mortal men,
But Mayas dream decline
She binds you to mortality.
I to Eternal life sublime.

Rejoice then when I come to you,
Each time at end of life.
It is to take you in my arms,
From worldly storms and strife.

Then with great lovingness and care
I'll put you at His feet
Beseech of Him your cyclic ego
Never to repeat.

Such are my humble services
I offer to mankind
Do I do this for recompense?
.......No!.....
It's just my love that's blind!

Karma

(A Soliloquy of Mind and Spirit)

I brushed aside the curtain
Of the window of mine eye
And beheld the sparkling Truth,
That within me did reply.
Oh Man you're not this house of flesh
Which sleeps decays and dies.
You are immortal consciousness,
King of the earth and skies.

Then burdened why am I,
With this coat of flesh and bone?
I questioned earnestly that Truth,
My very conscious home.
This coat your seed desire was,
Whose fruit is now your own.
Created by yourself you must,
Reap what you have sown.

Is this also the reason
For the hardships of my life?
Yes! Each cause has its relation
Just as Husband has a Wife.
Every action its reaction has,

With certainty that's True.
Do good works results of which,
Shall mould your life anew.

Pray tell me why the difference
Twixt the people on this earth?
Why do some have poverty
Some no financial dearth?
Why some sad and others gay
Some sick and others strong?
Is this the outcome of past deeds
Of personal right and wrong?

You've spoken well and seem to know
God's Mathmatical Law
All wrongs must be redressed indeed,
This fact it has no flaw.
All rights are rewarded
In proportion and no more.
To each one is meted out
His exact and proper score.

This unbribable Judge we people,
Call "The Karmic Law".
The supervisor of the Fates

Of our worldly see-saw
Who justly balances the ups
And downs of lives of man
Fitting the jigsaw of our fates
As we ourselves had planned.

What proof Hamsa Atman,
Can one get of his former karma?
The proof your own existence,
Circumstances and your dharma.
Your individual present,
Tells your reciprocal past.
As per their past desires,
People get their present task.

To the Truth is Truth begot,
The liar gets his own.
So make your actions such,
Whose reactions you don't moan.
To the likeness of your thinking,
Shall your character be made.
Dig deep your mind for noble thoughts,
With intellectual spade.

Oh Hamsa Spirit of my soul
What is my final goal?
Is there any such remedy to
Break this karmic hold?
This duality of opposites,
Teach me to override.
Take me with thee oh Spirit free,
On to the other side.

I am the Sun you are my ray,
You must become the whole.
By good conduct and service,
Your character shall mould.
By devotional meditation,
I – your spirit shall unfold.
The ray become the blazing Sun,
Yourself as Me behold!

Maya

Lo is he a waking dream
Or total fallacy?
Or is she just a game of time
In God's own fantasy?

    How strange this world of Maya is
    How gripping and how strong
    In this cosmic motion picture
    The right appears all wrong.

The false appears as truth
And the truth appears all false
On this Dancing dream of Maya
Is a paradoxical waltz.

    Then dance we must to nature's tune
    Of lust and fame and greed
    Until we realize its joys
    No more than sensual feed.

Yogiraj Gurunath

Discriminate Oh Brothers mine
Between reality and dream
Life is a passing caravan
It is not what it seems.

    Today we live throbbing with life.
    Tomorrow we are gone
    Mere shadows in a waking dream
    We leave this world forlorn.

Are you this house of flesh and bone
Swayed by the senses five?
Never, you are the light of God
The honey from his hive.

    You are the thinking principle
    Manushya you are called
    This body but a garment is
    In karmic web enthralled.

Manushay is the everlasting
Principal of man
Sharir delusive Mayas child
Of perishable man.

Arise Oh Children of the Lord.
Immortal souls Divine.
Break your delusive Mayic sleep,
Race for your home sublime.

Where supremest love doth reign
Sat-Chit-Ananda by name
Who ever was even is now
Will ever by the same.

Om Tat Sat Om
Om Tat Sat Om

Yogiraj Gurunath

Hamsa Still

[The philosophy of enlightened action]

Opal Hamsa of the mystic skies
From whose bosom doth thou rise?
Where to where do flight you take
What fathomless Truth you awake !

I have no birth nor death in time
Unborn awake I never sleep
Kundali is the self-born Me
Moving creation from the deep !

My true self is the selfless Self
I came to be by Being !
Pulling the veil of Maya
By my will I am the Hamsa Still

Hamsa Eternal how may we
Being work-bound yet be everfree?
Enlightened action is the key
Which gives that final liberty!

Action from desires of the seeds
Of past or future thoughts
Creates a Karmic bondage which
Is ceaselessly with troubles fraught.

Enlightened action doth arise
Within your crystal conscious skies
Experience of the Hamsa Still
Make you know Divinity's will

Mind Transformation

As a leaking vessel never can fill
Waters of Life so pure and still
So distracted mind fails to retain
Wisdom's nectar in its brain

> To fill waters from wisdom's spring
> Our minds we must to stillness bring
> Then our crystal bowl of tranquil mind
> With Gnosis fills of supernal kind

But if the very thoughts of mind
Be as fleeting deer and hind
Darting wayward ways they find
Such men to wisdom's ways are blind

> To ease disease of random mind
> A remedy suitable we must find
> A rhythmic breathing tension free
> With absorption the sovereign key

Steady poise the arrow your will
And shoot the fleeting mind to still
The deer of thoughts, hinds & harts
Felled by your concentrated darts

    As one by one they die away
    Mind opens up to new day
    Streams run tranquil willows sway
    Here tame and gentle deer do play

Tamed and tuned to natures flow
Mind melts into the opal glow
Which radiates from the soul within
Where Wisdom's mystic fire is king !

Mystic Wine

The Bishop's Wine

Oh the Bishop's Wine by far the best
Old Vintage wine; a cut above the rest
Only he knows how to mature it best
And patiently his time invest.

Time spent in solitude of mind
Enrichens wine of any kind
Where silence stills the finest brew
That vintage tastes like honey dew.

In vermilion vestry of his mind
Brew exotic grapes of rarest kind
He culls the grape fruits fragrant Heart
No palate can ever find!

Then vermilion vintage he prepares
Within himself with breath as yeast
Ferments textured wine of sparkling zest;
Oh! The Bishop's wine by far the best!

Each day is holy communion day
For a Bishop of my mindless stay
I drink I'm drunk I drift away
A euphoria blows me heavens way

The holy grail my crystal thought
Holds my vermilion wine sublime
I sip I seep humanity's heart
Knowing it to be my heart at large!

From sanctum-torium drop by drop
Tongue soaks elixir's wine sublime.
Lulls me to ecstasy's rosy rest
Oh! The Bishop's wine by far the best

Hallelujah Christ is risen today
Wake up Bishop, it's Easter day
Your wine has had its winning way
Hosannas here with us to stay!

Yogiraj Gurunath

ODE TO SURYA

(A Solar Meditation)

I drink oh drink thee Sun of Life
Your roaring radiance rinse me through
Gushing through spine with Sizzling joy
I thy Divinity enjoy!

Form thy elysian fountain rays
I drink immortal Pranic Life
Rejuven Body and my mind
Dissolve all worldly woe and strife!

Dancing with thine immortal light
Each cell suffused with joy of Life
I glorify this gift oh Lord
No Emperor ever can afford!

Orange elixirs wine sublime
Flows glows in every fiber mine
Filling me with thy Bliss sublime
Making me to My Self Divine!

16

Déjà Vu

Wild flowers so fresh in life
Breeze through alleys of my mind
Fragrancing memories of the past
In mountain lakes reflections cast

In wooded valleys berries crushed
The flavor of the mystic musk
Within me did old memories rise
Devotions to the sunset skies

Forest aroma deep in damp
Wild smell of the wooded pines
Oh ! the déjà vu of jungle times
Of long past meditations lives

Where in sylvan bowers I sat
Not in this world nor in that
Just in the joy of Selfing mirth
The odor of the fragrant earth !

My mind a laughing gurgling stream
Running the bedrocks mossy green
Becomes a calm meandering dream
Flowing into Myself serene

17

My melting mind a flowing stream
Entered the rainbow ocean light
There was no fear nor sorrows night
Except awareness and delight

How long I sat there no one knows
The eventide its shadows cast
In many a sunrise rays I basked
No one came nor ever asked

The trivial round the common task
Meditation then to me became
A natural mind in tune so tame
Transcending frivolous name and fame

Just being quiet was so good
A lying log, a forest wood
Moving with the natural breeze
Amidst the deep dark forest trees

With body dead consciousness live
Expanding in eternal skies
Beyond mayas conditioned dream
The self merging in Self supreme.

My Cup of Tea

The morning sunshine on my back
Gentle breezes blowing through
Gold brown books on the old wood rack
Oh! My steaming cup of tea that brew!

From which mysteriously did spring
Nostalgic memories old and new
Wafting my mind aloft and light
To another worldly inner flight

Of mystic flavors colors too
Of which never ever knew
Yet somehow from my inner most Being
I experienced True what I was seeing

A Bliss experienced oft before
It satisfied my innermost core
Knowing it to be myself and more
Of my own larger treasure store

All things were made of spiritual light
Swans lake to lake in glorious flight

Fainting fragrance Lotus bloomed
In this Paradise the mind was doomed

Thoughts die dissolve to live in knowing
That boundless consciousness all growing
In ever expanding Love and Joy
All things of matter but a toy

A figment of the conscious Self
Conditioned mind a sneaky elf
Of negativity in time
Was transformed to Gnosis sublime

Heard it but I didn't hear
The dog barking so far so near
In the backyard chasing hens
Fluttering hither to the fence

The neighboring housewife I beheld
Brisk and about her daily chores
Washing dishes cleaning floor
Sweeping in and out of doors

Yet all my consciousness was me
In spite of all this revelry
Immersed in my awareness me
Bound to worldly task yet Free

*Fame nor position matter
To one's inner life of peace
Virtues used as virtues sake
Cause all sorrows to cease*

Autobiography of the Self

•

*Boundless lay the Self existent
in the Paramartha of the Self,
Spread beyond Infinity, from Eternity to Eternity,
was perfect absolute and calm;
calm undisturbed, for
Creation was not yet conceived of the Creator
who in the stillness of His Majesty did reign.*

Parinishpanna art though Oh All-in-All,
Not this, Not this thou art,
the essence of all light and dark
There was no darkness then,
there even was no light
There was no action then to cause reaction, all was
Thyself ineffable and endless consciousness of Bliss

For then in nothing was the everything,
in everything was nothing
These feeble words seek humbly
to express Thy majesty Para Brahman
For even Absolute is limited
to the Oh ineffable peace
That passeth all understanding.

TRUTH, the life of Prana lay potential in Thee,
Oh All-In All
Time was not, Space was not,
Creation there was none.
Yet Oh Supreme, all were held
in Thy bosom of Duration
The Lord of LIGHT had not awakened but reposed in
Thee.

The Eternal Spark had not impulsed
to set causation in motion;
Then would the birth of creation begin
in Relative Sequence
And Maha Maya would go forth
in her celestial dance
Creating Countless universes and galaxies to Thy Glory.

If at one time, at the same place,
that very moment
The sunburst of a countless suns occur.
That brilliance would scarce suffice to show Thy shadow
What must be Thy light!
Darker than the darkest hell; more glorious than Brahma
Lok art Thee
Thy splendor knows no majesty.

Lo! Thou didst exhale Thy universal Self,
Oh Calm
and Thy Infinite Mind Oh Lord
did make the mighty Lord of Flame
Who exploding in His Light
did Maya's Creation ignite
To set the Wheel of Creation in Motion, Maya's Motion.

*The eternal Mother Adi-Shakti then did make her galaxies
and other relative aspects of creation did begin,
The Sound Sublime, creator of causation space and time
did originate in Thy bosom Oh Thou
Mula-Prakriti of Light
Resounding in every substance
of creation Thy organ Oooommmm!*

Then Light and heat and moisture,
they were born of Thee
Oh! Mother Adi-Shakti,
Vast Nebulae of light and heat did float
the spaces infinite to regulate themselves into galaxies
Then by Myriad Permutation Combinations Mother
Did Thou form the Suns and Stars in Thy immortal Song.

Great masses of vibrating incandescent light were stars
So large as to stagger human imagination
Mother really dost though wear such jewels on Thy breast?
And still find time to love us mortal children so far below
Oh Bhagavati,
in every molecule Thy love it glows and grows.

These mighty vapors of Light and the Stars they stud Thy brow
Oh Thou Mother of Eternal Light Thy glory knows no night
These children galaxies of Thine, these Stellar Solar systems hold;
in perfect harmony they move,
all held by that force
Oh Mother we mortals call Thy Radh,
Thy gravitational love.

Then came the Sons of light - of Shakti they were born,
Blazing in their power and truth they worked
through worlds and stars and fraught
cooling the hot, heating the cold, moistening the dry
and perfecting in their harmony all undue disharmony to
set about the perfect evolution
of the Worlds of Mortal man.

The Cyclic Motion of Creation then began,
it was causation's dance in relative Oceans
The day came on and gave birth unto the night
The breeze raced over vast tracts of solid lands
and liquid waters
did their position take in hollows of the earth.

*Sacred Bhumi oh Mother World Thou art; the essence of
Adi-Shakti;
To Thee, by whose womb we mortals were born
our endless salutations to Thee
Oh Thou divine spouse of Vishnu, our eternal Lord
Our Universe of Endless stars lives their lifes in Thee
Only so long as Thou dost wish them to be.*

Oh Bhumi Ma, Thy chosen child was Vasundhara
Who came to be so that she may mother her
mortal living Man.
Then did begin the evolution of the future Man
that spark of life divine entered the mineral rock,
its first primeval home.
For the spark was of Vasundhara the Child of Bhumi
Who in turn was of Adi-Shakti Parameswari.

And Mother Adi-Shakti, one with Mula-Prakritri was of the Essence of Parinishpanna, our Supreme Paramatma. Then that spark of life was also of the Paramatma in the relative sense.
There was nothing not of Paramatma, the Supreme Purusha.

Yogiraj Gurunath

The spark divine grew from the mineral rock into the plant
Wherein it did flourish,
then dying out from the plant the Spark of life
was born into the fish and then the mammals.
I died from the lower tabernacle of matter
to enter a more expressive One.

I died out from the rock to live in the plant.
I died out from the plant to live in the fish and reptile.
I died from reptile to live in animal and lastly
I died out from the animal house of flesh to enter the
house of man. Wherein did I become the lessor by dying?
For dying was another form of life.

And all along Evolution's path did I travel,
My outer coats were different,
each one more expressive than the first
but essentially I was the same.
And finally awaited me the most crucial temple, Man
But it was only a man of clay, until I entered my ray.

I entered into the flesh of man as ray of light,
the thinking light,
I was that consciousness who came from the Supreme.
My Light gave the house of flesh to know
that I was a glow the child of light.
The Ego it was formed by me for future generations to be
the thinking principle they know as mind
which is the essence of all Mankind.

I came into the physical house of man,
to rule over that Tabernacle of flesh,
but was deluded by the Satanic desires of the Flesh
into thinking I was a body and not the light.
This Heresy of separateness covered my sight,
forgetting I was potentially divine,
Maya's veil covered that spark to haunt me in the
darkness of body flesh.

Then man looked up to the portending stars
to question whether they his life did make.
The stars looked down, smiled and replied
"Son, nothing can Thy Immortal Essence take."
Then girding up His Loins the cave man did begin
his upward evolution aspiring to be one with
Him who is in all and break Mayic illusion.

*Oh Maya Thou nature's eve, Thou didst hide from my
Manus Self,
my Father Self the Atman Buddhi.
Then my struggle of life began
to unite Manus that was me
to my Father Atma Buddhi and Jivan mukta to be;
The Cyclic ego then began its rounds of reincarnations.*

It did repeat itself till Manu's Son
vanquished Satanic Maya
and did become one with father Atma-Buddhi.
Who essentially one with Paramartha was
The Father Atma, Mother Buddhi and
Manu's Child being one.
The deluded Manusputra had regained his lost birth-right
and entered into his Father -Mother bosom of Light.

The fallen state regained: Lo!
Behold the lesser ones to come.
The lower animals had to struggle up.
Oh Sons of light help them! Guide them!
The plants, the rocks must be evolved
for in all was the essential spark of Atman.
The Paramatmic Divine Self must help
the Jivatmic human Self.
This is the Cosmic Law.

The molecules in each mineral substance did contain
vast quantity of atoms, each representing
a miniature Solar System.
All rotating revolving and evolving
as per a preplanned power
That ineffable mighty essence of the Self Atma.
From the Vastest Nebulae to the Atoms smallest spray
did He in His own majesty parade.

The Spirit was the essence of the All, both big and small,
Hot and cold, light and dark did contain
that one essential spark.
Even the minute electron contained its essence positrons
that were composed of measons whose energy children
lifetrons traveled through the breath of man.

But finer than the lifetrons of Prana was the
Essence of God-thought,
one with the all-pervading Spirit, the Atman.
There was no segregation in this Spirit of God-thought,
For from this the dream fabric of Maya
was composed and made
It was the vastest infinity of Divinity.

From the essential substance of God thought
the Sun and the Moon and the Stars were built,
Stellar and Solar Systems also had their sway
because God thought was in them to stay.
All was of God's thought
and God-thought was One thought,
The divine thought of the universal oneness of Eternity.

For being the subtlest of the all from it was made the all;
It was the smallest of the small for beyond human
imagination.
Would it then be correct to call that God-thought non-
Being?
And thereby express its absolute entirety over creation in
Being?

The All-being was the God-thought which was
the essential essence of every atom of creation.
The all being was the God-thought
Self-existent in Eternity.
The Self that all pervading
consciousness of stillness through eternity
Composed of nothing yet of which all else is sure composed,
It stands supreme beyond all dreams eternally reposed.

Spirit is the God-thought, there is nothing it is not.
The All is One, the One is all, the All-in All Paramartha,
Oh, Absolute Majesty of sublimest existence,
Oh ineffable peace beyond human understanding,
Our ceaseless salutation to Thee
who ever was, even is now and shall forever be.

Let not precious moments slip by
Seek now ! the ultimate truth
Jivahamsa spread your wings to fly
Immortal realms which death defy

MY MOTHER OF RENUNCIATION

I am thy child, Oh Panna Dai,
a countless deaths I'll die for thee
Oh Mother of True sacrifice,
Thy courage knows no majesty.

> I love thee more than all the Mothers
> past and yet to be
> Give me thy courage Ma and
> teach me how a Tyagi I must be.

What greater courage could
a nursing Mother ever show
Than sacrifice her very throbbing
blood and heart and soul.

> Oh Mother, Thou didst wrench me
> from thy breast I had not drunk
> That love I so much craved you kept,
> I empty did depart.

Thy urge to give me nectar of thy love,
it was so strong
That 'ere my lips had left thy breast
thy love it did gush forth.

Then from thy breast did Maya flow,
and heart renunciations glow
Thy milk did drench thy clothes Oh Ma,
and dripping sadly to the floor it begged

"Leave me not my Child for thee
I love much more than me."
But Mothers blood of sacrifice
rebuked her very milk and cried.

"Hold me not back to renounce
every molecule and ounce of love,
For I must give so that the Nation's
countless children, they may live."

But Mother you still owe me love
which is by birthright mine
From you I have to learn as yet
the Greatest lesson of all time.

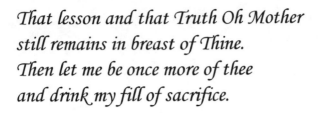

That lesson and that Truth Oh Mother
still remains in breast of Thine.
Then let me be once more of thee
and drink my fill of sacrifice.

Oh Panna Dai, that which was thine
was also ever mine
That milk of sacrifice and Tyag had courage
and had love Divine.

Not even bravest of the brave
can teach me to renounce
Only from thy mayic milk I'll learn
to break all Maya's bounds.

My heart in thee, Thy soul in me
such oneness did us bind
Then How did you my loving heart
surpass all humankind?

The pain of separation was much more
for thee than twas for me
Bhagvati of Tyag art thou,
who else could bear such agony.

Yes Mother now I know,
none else than Bhagvati art thou
To sacrifice your heart and blood,
the kingdom's honor to restore.

I felt thee gently with firm hands
lay me in my death bed
The brute did stab his steel in me
and Mother's love ran red.

That blood which flowed with love of Tyag,
it glowed.
My Mother's blood,
the highest of renunciation showed.

I thought by giving me to death
you had left me and gone
But little did I know Oh Ma,
death was your other form.

Then I let my body go even
as a snake leaves slough
To enter once again into
my Mother's conscious womb and glow.

Upon strength of such sacrifice a
re myriad heroes born.
My ceaseless salutations are to thee,
My Mother, and my all.

Thy manifested Self Oh Ma
in form and flesh was Panna Dai
Thy Self in true they only knew
who passed the gates of death in time.

Koti Koti Pranams
Koti Koti Pranams

Prayer to Kundalini Divine

Hiss Kundali sting ego mine
With nectar poison so sublime
Piercing my rainbow Lotus shrines
Making me to myself divine !

Kundalini bless me with thy blaze
Delusion, suffering fear efface
Spine darkness; with they lightening light
Fragrance me ! Negative karma ignite !

You are livingness ! its Life you keep
Oh Mother of the mystic deep !
Remove shadow of death from me
In Shiva deathlessly to be !

Yogi

Living in Calm and Solitude
Subduing body and his Mind
Within himself in gratitude
Ridding Desires of all Kind.

Neath Sylvan bowers in his Seat
Cool Stream flows by deerskin laid neat
This is the Yogi's true retreat
In meditation is his treat.

The Asans selected best are two
For him to meditation do
The first Padmasana lotus trance
Then Siddhasana the perfect stance.

Yogi's in Dhyan become aware
How breath at birth did them ensnare
Twenty one thousand thirty score
Japa leads soul to salvation's door.

Yogiraj Gurunath

In Padmasan do bandh trine
Focus on Kundalini in spine
Practice breathing Pran-apan
Know precious Kundalini Gyan.

By Hard Practice sweat beads form
Rub them into the body form
Then Yogi must of milk avail
Avoid all food, acid and stale.

Food is energy for the mind
And goes to mental making
Soft sweets and fruits oh! Yogi eat
At every fast of breaking

For psychic nerves to Purify
One must move both sun and moon
And all humours is us to dry
We must perfect maha-mudra try

Hamsa is Gayatri's ajapa japa
Opener of Yogi's heavenly door
Breathing with awareness let him strive
And let not him his animal drive

From Kundali is Hamsa born
Flowing is spine as Pran-apan
Yogi's stilling the Pran-apan
Are true adepts in sama Dhyan.

This knowledge is all supreme
It's practice melts the magic dream
Experience of the "Hamsa Still"
Makes Us know Divinity's will.

Oh valiant Yogi striving free
By pranic kumbak break the seal
The Brave by storm the heaven's take
Nirvan through kundali they make

Having blocked with her face
The path leading to Shiva's shrine
Awake! Oh Kundalini mine
And lead me to my home divine!

The Yogic Prana ablaze unites
With Kundalini to ignite
Mind intellect then penetrate
Sukhma chakras living light

She like a hissing serpent goes
Glistening kundali upward flows
By magnet heat of Pranayam
Awaken's she! Our wisdom grows.

Your own meat swallow yogi
Get drunk with inner wine
The profane value these secrets not
Cast not your pearls before the swine.

By Allakh Gorakhia's mystic touch
Disease hunger not sleep assail
Yogis who rent mayas death veil
Are those who in khechari prevail

By afflictions is he troubled not
Nor tainted by his fruits of karma
Is troubled not by sting of death
He Mrityunjay conqueror of breath

Take padmasana perfect pose
In lush serene surrounding
Shivnetra Yogi lost in OM
Know self as sound Resounding

Om thou creative light divine
In all the seven heavens shine
Lightless light of all the light
Sun moon and fire you ignite

    In the Blueprint of creation
    Emblazoned is thy cosmic seal
    Causation space & time are but
    Projections of your magic dream

Om with every breath & thought
Sets yogi free from karma
Giving Nirvana to striving souls
As per their own swadharms

    Even the evil chanting 'Om'
    Are tainted not by karma
    They will be like a lotus lying
    Unwet in water and undying

Absorbed in Om, the semen stills
By ceaseless Pranayama
Lifeprana is still, semen is still
Conquer death, new life fulfill

As long as pran in body flows
The soul therein doth reside
Pran leaves, soul also body leaves
So live for God! Do Pranayam

To ward off kala death they say
Gods and sages in Pranayam stay
Yogi puts death's fear away
And lives in prana the kevali way

Deathless Yogi, fearless bold
Prana between the eyebrows hold
By kevali in Shivanetra be!
Oh death where is they victory?

In lotus posture yogi stay
Do sun-moon prana of night & day
Spinal breathing it is called
Victor of death be breath enthralled

He stands supreme beyond all dream
Of friend and foe alike
Success 'n failure, name and fame
To Him a mere dolls wedding game

Satisfied with what he has
Bathing in wisdom's fountain head
Conqueror of the senses five
He drinks the honey from his hive

In joy and sorrow light & dark
He ever that eternal spark
In honour and dishonour too
The constant yogi ever new!

The well-made mind is Self alone
Its wrongs need no atone
Because the well-made mind shall soar
Above karmic effect and flaw

Established in the Self he glows
Beyond intelligence he flow's
Transcending all the senses five
In the "here-now!" Truth alive

Beholding self by Self supreme
Shattering the waking dream
Maya shall be put to flight
By those who in the Self delight

Yogiraj Gurunath

A Compassionate & healing light
A Hamsa in its splendid flight
Away oh darkness! Fly oh night!
The Yogi comes in radiant might.

Allak Niranjan Om Shiv Om!!
Allak Niranjan Om Shiv Om!!

REALITY

This world is but a thoughtfulness
of Mayic atoms intertwined
Whose electrons are energy
of light essence sublime.

    Newton rediscovered and
    declared the Laws of Motion
    Sir Apple fell for Eve before
    and then for Gravitation

Cause and effect are bound to be
one with nature's duality
Oscillating within the laws
of Mayas' karmic causality.

    What physics and what chemistry
    their laws must have corollary
    Action reaction, attraction repulsion,
    cause and effect are bound to be.

" Laws of creation subject are
  to equilibrium forces.
This world in balance cannot be
without its gains and losses."

There is no day without its night,
nor cause without effect
For attraction must repulsion be
just as for life is death.

The Einstein based his theory
on hypothesis of light
Relating all that matters
to finality of light.

But the Krishna and the Christ perceived
light to be form of energy.
Emanating from the omniscient mind
that one cosmic reality.

They further saw that energy
was not the final law.
It was a grosser consciousness
but that too had its flaw.

This world our sages did perceive
is mindstuff materialized.
In relative sequence it is built
deceiving mortal eyes.

All that is composed they knew
must get decomposed
Where then does reality lie?
All matter being composed.

That all pervading consciousness
of stillness through Eternity
Must of necessity proclaim
its ultimate reality.

Composed of nothing yet of which
all else is sure composed
It stands supreme beyond all dreams
eternally reposed.

That one cosmic reality
is spirit they perceived
Whose omnipresent essence
is everlasting bliss.

Whose one dream atom
doth our universe contain
Its myriad worlds and planets
He doth orderly maintain.

To This Everlasting Truth of Love,
This Infinite Divinity
Countless creations homage pay
throughout His Own Eternity.

DEDICATED TO SHIV GORAKSHA NATH BABAJI

Who art Thou?
I know Thee not and yet I am of Thee
I cannot comprehend thee,
Oh Thou Emperor of Divinity.

> *I sit and melt in silence of*
> *Thy Love Oh Infinite.*
> *Make me thy Truth,*
> *Make me thy Love*
> *Eternal Lord of Light*

Countless creations do you make
Goraksha Nath Divine
A thought projected by you
Makes causation, space and time

There never was a Sage or Saint
Who was not born of Thee
Thou art the essence of their Souls
Divine Paramatma Free

We Jivatmas also Lord
Have our birth and being in Thee
The Thou must also be in us
Supremest Monarchy.

How shall I love Thee Babaji?
Words are so dry and dumb
I can't express Thy majesty
My intellect runs numb.

My heart it bursts oh all in all
To love Thee endlessly
But Lord I cannot bring to words
I'm tongue-tied hopelessly.

Give me the strength to shout Thy love
Across the seven seas
Deludging this world with light
For infinite eternities.

In solitudes of my mind
My devotion it dost burst to hear
Thy song immortal song of love
Thou everlasting Seer.

As long as darkness covers me
And ignorance doth do us part
So long in agony I'll be
Striving to be with Thee my Heart.

Through pain and hunger I shall strive
To touch Thy feet oh Lord
It matters not if bones or body
Perish in this battle fort.

I'm burning in My love for Thee
Eternal infinite
I cannot rest in peace now
Till I do become thy Light.

In silent supplications
I do burn and yearn to be in Thee
Hear Thou my soul cry
Break my bonds Babaji
Set me free.

81

Set me free to be in Thee
Let there be none of me
Then me in Thee
Thy love in me
I shall become of Thee.

Pleasures nor palaces exude
That Bliss of peaceful solitude
Attunement with the Self alone
Gives that final beatitude !

Sat Guru Bhakti

From the Guru's feet flows the
spiritual river Ganga
Which washes all the sins of my Heart
Oh Shiva when shall my relationship
With you become one?

    The love that flows from the Guru's Eyes
    Saturates my body with Nectar.
    Oh Shiva when shall my relationship
    With you become one?

The Guru's blessing flame awakens me
And opens the eyes of my heart and soul
Oh Shiva when shall my soul be
Merged in Thy eternal Spirit?

    A blinding light in my mental sky
    May I behold Shiv Goraksha
    All my binding shackles of Karma are broken

One with Shiva I have become
All my attachments are broken
And One with Shiva I have become.

ALAK NIRANJAN KAR SHIVOM!
ALAK NIRANJAN KAR SHIVOM!

Thy Love Lives Oh Christ

Who feels Thy love Beloved Christ,
it spreads into eternity
It permeates each atom
our existing Humanity.

    Each fibre in my body and
    my innermost spirit yearns for Thee
    In what fashion shall I Lord!
    Express my burning love for Thee.

Words are too callous and too dry
to touch thy ineffable Love Divine.
Speak to me Jesus in my heart
and tell me Thou art mine.

    Such is the depth and warmth of
    Thy ineffable love divine.
    Speak to me Jesus in my heart
    and tell me thou art mine.

Tell me Oh Christ; That I am Thine
I ask for nothing more
Beyond all riches and all fame
do I Thy love adore.

Oh Messiah of the humble and
the meek and pure in heart
I yearn to be absorbed
in Thee never to depart.

While suffering pangs on cross of death;
Divinity it spoke from you
"Father forgive these children
for they know not what they do".

Was there a loftier love phrase
ever uttered by mankind?
Saying this Thou didst depart,
leaving Thy body coat behind.

Oh King of Yogis little did
these blinded children know
That Thou were master of
Thy body and its passing show!

Then brighter than brilliance itself
on Easter Thou didst rise
To show the Light of love divine
to blinded mortal eyes.

Then Heaven and earth rejoiced
for the Spirit of the Lord
Had filled creation with its love
and struck through Thee that cord.

That cord of Love which doth vibrate
the human fibre up to date
And make us cry with love and joy:
Hosanna in the Highest!

Hari Om Tat Sat Om

Samadhi

O Thou phantom of creation's song
Why did you keep me tied so long?

    This nature's Eve, she can't deceive
    The people pure and strong
    For they in God's own light perceive
    The truth where they belong.

I stop this breath,
my stillness enters
Into the velvety darkness
of death.

    I grow
    in consciousness sublime
    Engulfing countries,
    continents and time.

I further grow
in omniscient glow
To unite with
maya's karmic flow.

The subtle laws
of cause and effect
Within myself
I do detect.

Beyond the gates of death!
I glide – untied;
Into regions sublime – surpassing
causation space and time.

Here Eternal Bliss is King
by name of Sat Chit Anand
Whose Life Sublime of Truth Divine
is Loving Brahmanand.

I fill immensity of space – I am
the Self Supreme
Looking down I do perceive
creation as a dream.

I then blend in the everlasting
vast expanse of Light
Becoming one with the
Cosmic Hum of all resounding
Oooommmmm.

Joy of Festivals in Dhyan

An outsider here, I belong to a country
Where there is no life nor death
All 12 months I drink the divine elixir (Amrit)
Which awakens me to Self
Soul and dissolves my ego.
Oh Divine! My very being is ego's non being!

A foreigner to this land my true home belongs,
Where the blossoms of spring bloom every day;
In this body garden the 7 lotuses bloom
To adorn the lotus feet of Goraksha Nath.
Oh Soul! The lotuses become
the arches of the Divine feet!

A foreigner to this land I belong to a country
Where the festival of colours (Holi)
is celebrated each day.
There sprayed with 7 colours I am transformed
Whirling in festive joy I become (colourless) pure
white.
Oh! Brother oblivious of my ego & body.

An outsider here my true country is
Where there is perpetual irradiant splendour
Seven coloured wheels
        of mystic fire swirl within me
And every day is the festival of Divali (lights).

An outsider here the country
I belong to is where the music of
The 36 soothing ragas is heard
At Dessaraha the big drum sounds Nada Brahm
And the Ragas reverberate the Omkar.

I am a dweller of that boundless country
Where Lord Goraksha is King of all souls.
There he breathes the Ham Sah
we are being breathed
He does the work all sit at rest
Oh! Brother we all sit in tranquillity.

I am a dweller of that divine land
Which is called the Param Dhaia (Supreme Abode)
Siddha Nath is my name
My place town of rest
is Amrit Ghat (nectar vessel above third eye).

ALAKH NIRANJAN KAR SHIV OM

Yogiraj Gurunath

APPENDIX

Yogiraj Sat Gurunath

A brief introduction to his teachings

His Life

Yogiraj Sat Gurunath was born on May 10th, 1944. He is a Siddha by birth and belongs to one of the premier families of Gwalior, India. Educated in Sherwood College [Nainital], he spent his early years in the Himalayas with the great Nath Yogis, in whose presence he was transformed. The *Divine Transformation* was completed by his deep and personal experience with Mahavtar Babaji (*Shiv Goraksha Nath Babaji*)

Yogiraj now teaches various ancient forms of Yoga founded by the Nath Tradition, such as Mahavatar Babaji Kriya Yoga. He bestows powerful Shaktipat transmissions and unique No-mind Sates of awareness which empower the practitioners to gradually go into Sahaj Samadhi (awareness of one's own Self), experiencing the depth of Eternal Being. *Lord Krishna's* vision has given him to realize the oneness of all yogas, faiths and religions.

His Genius

Besides the Himalayan Masters, Sat Gurunath is the only Siddha known to us and broadly accessible, who gives authentic experiences of **Kundalini Energy Transmission** created specifically for spiritual and healing transformation essential to the awakening and continued evolution of humankind. The sincere will receive these dimensions of the Guru's consciousness through **direct experience** as to what true yoga is rather than through intellectual exploration. The experience of Sat Gurunath's Consciousness will be bestowed as the Guru guides the seeker in transforming his thought-filled finite mind into infinite consciousness free of thoughts.

Herein lies the **Genius of Gurunath**, with a flash he bestows upon you His Consciousness of Natural Enlightenment, transforming the ripples of thought in your mind's lake into a waveless lake of Soul Awareness bereft of thought. With flawless clarity during this passage he keeps intact the awareness of ones individual self as the boundaries of it's I-ness melt into the knowing of one's own boundless Awareness.

The mind's I-ness will attempt to its own expansion into higher knowledge out of fear of losing its own identity. But this is only half the truth. The complete truth is that the individual mind loses its identity only to partake its vaster identity as infinite awareness, the drop merges into the ocean not to lose itself but to become of it.

The Uniqueness of Gurunath is that with utter simplicity by breathing through us he brings to you Shiv Goraksha Babaji's Kriya Yoga and the Timeless Yoga of the Nath Yogis. He has simplified the arduous Nath techniques, yet preserved the effectiveness of the sacred practices. As a living master, he offers to humanity his own clear-mind consciousness. In sharing this experience with each individual seeker personally and with thousands of receptive people the world over simultaneously, Sat Gurunath reveals the secret that at the level of pure consciousness all **Humanity is One.**

The Nath Lineage of Kriya Yoga

As we peer into the akashic records of the misty past we get a glimpse of the lineage of the Nath Yogis. It began from Adi Nath, Lord Shiva Himself, who gave it to His consort Parvati, Uday Nath. She gave it to Vishnu Santosh Nath, Ganesh and Nandi Nath. Then Lord Krishna as Vishnu initiated Lord Vivasat, the Spirit of our Sun. The lineage was later guarded by the Kings of the Solar Dynasty: Vaivasat Manu, King Ikshavaku down to Harishchandra, then to Lord Raghu Nath (Rama), 47th in descent from Ikshavaku. He is the 8th Rudra, esoterically connected with Shiv Goraksha Babaji, who is an incarnation of Lord Shiva Himself. It is through this grand lineage of the Nath Yogis that the royal science of Kriya Yoga has been preserved and handed down through the corridors of time by the ever-living Shiv Goraksha Babaji. It is to this lineage that Yogiraj Gurunath belongs – blessed by Babaji to spread this divine science in the East and West.

His Hallmark : The Knowing of a True Master

A Satguru or Empowering Master can be known by three distinct graces he bestows upon his disciples.

1. Transmit – center to center in their pranic chakras – the evolutionary Kundalini Energy.

2. Breathe the powerful breath through the breathing of disciples in their Spinal channels.

3. Impart this consciousness of natural enlightenment to the receptive

    Only a Master who showers all three blessings on truth seekers is a true Satguru. Gurunath bestows all three blessings.

Spiritual Evolution As taught by Gurunath

Wings to Freedom – The Journey of the Soul

The way of the white swan is the evolution of human consciousness, the most comprehensive enterprise ever undertaken by humanity, besides which the greatest of human achievements pale into insignificance. This process is Yoga, which commends itself to the foremost minds of East and West. In the human brain exists the lateral ventricles in the shape of a "Swan in Flight" with its head pointing to the back as though the swan is flying faster than light back to the future. When the Hamsa Yogi, through meditation and pranayam, activates the Kundalini energy, then these ventricles in the brain open up. The two petals in the Agya Chakra, corresponding to the pituitary gland, open. The Yogi, at this

96

stage, experiences Hamsa Consciousness, being breathed by the Divine Indweller.

The Sushumna channel in the spinal chord is the highway through which the Kundalini Energy travels and the evolution of consciousness takes place. It is the kinetic energy remaining after the completion of the universe. This force lies as light/sound vibrations potentially coiled around the swayambhu linga in the mooladhar chakra. To avail of it for one's own evolution and realization is the birthright of every human soul. It may be awakened by yogic procedures - best by Unmani, a no-mind state of absorption.

As the Hamsa Nath Yogi progresses in the Hamsa meditation, the third eye opens up in the Agya Chakra and he goes into the Sarvikalpa consciousness. Then, by further practice, he penetrates the Star of the Eye and expands to the Paramhansa Nath Yogi state of Nirvikalpa consciousness, dwelling in the Cave of Brahma[1], the brain's third ventricle. Then his awareness evolves further beyond the I-ness of humanity to settle in the lateral swan-like ventricles of the brain, where he becomes the Siddha Nath Yogi. The mighty Hamsa soul has won its wings to freedom. As the subtle fibers of the Corona Radiata light up with Divine effulgence he takes flight into Cosmic consciousness as the Avadhoot Nath Yogi. He experiences

the total Divinity of and beyond creation, gaining the ultimate knowledge of "Tat Tvam Asi" "That Thou Art". The Yogi then merges into Niranjan, the final Nirvana, having attained the enlightenment of Buddha and Christ. This Avadhoot Nath Yogi returns to the world no more. If, under rare circumstances, he ever does, it will be the descent of Divinity as Avatar Nath Yogi.

Vision for World Peace

If World Peace is to Herald the Dawn of New Age, realize that

Humanity One's Only Religion

Breath One's Only Prayer and

Consciousness One's Only God

Yogiraj Sat-Gurunath

Hamsa Yoga Sangh — a non-profit world-wide mission foundered by Gurunath

In order to further his vision for Earth Peace and the Evolution of Human Consciousness, Yogiraj Sat Gurunath founded Hamsa Yoga Sangh, a non-profit organization. It currently runs centers in India, Switzerland and the United States.

Mission Statement :

Hamsa Yoga Sangh's mission is to serve humanity. In so doing, it is

· **Meditated** to the furthering of human awareness for earth peace.

· **Dedicated to serving humanity as one's larger self...**

· **Committed** to making yours and others lives a happiness.

It offers a variety of opportunities to interested people and provides a community of care and support for sincere truth seekers.

The Meaning of Hamsa Yoga Sangh

Hamsa Yoga Sangh's name consists of three important aspects of Yogiraj's teachings and practices:

Hamsa is the Swan of Life and symbolizes the Soul. The incoming and outgoing breath in man are the two wings of the Swan. When a Yogi unites his mind with the inflow and outflow of his casual breath he enters the natural state of *Sahaj Samadhi*. The mystic meaning of Hamsa is "I am merged with the Divine."

Yoga is union in Samadhi.

It is an inner ascent through evermore refined and evermore expanded spheres of consciousness, towards a realization of the Godessence which lies at the core of one's own being. Yoga is Composed Mind.

Sangh is a collective Awareness of Souls.

It is a collective awareness of souls travelling along the passage of time, evolving till they merge into the Divine, the drop partaking of the ocean of Consciousness.